YA
B
Dar

Sneddon, Bradley.

Charles Darwin.

SCIENTISTS AND THEIR DISCOVERIES

CHARLES DARWIN

SCIENTISTS AND THEIR DISCOVERIES

SCIENTISTS AND THEIR DISCOVERIES
CHARLES DARWIN

BRADLEY SNEDDON

MASON CREST

YA
B
Dar
01/19/21
ls 1/20

Mason Crest
450 Parkway Drive, Suite D
Broomall, Pennsylvania 19008
(866) MCP-BOOK (toll-free)
www.masoncrest.com

Copyright © 2019 by Mason Crest, an imprint of National Highlights, Inc.

Printed and bound in the United States of America.

CPSIA Compliance Information: Batch #SG2018.
For further information, contact Mason Crest at 1-866-MCP-Book.

First printing
9 8 7 6 5 4 3 2 1

Library of Congress Cataloging-in-Publication Data

ISBN: 978-1-4222-4028-1 (hc)
ISBN: 978-1-4222-7760-7 (ebook)

Scientists and their Discoveries series ISBN: 978-1-4222-4023-6

Developed and Produced by National Highlights Inc.
Interior and cover design: Yolanda Van Cooten
Production: Michelle Luke

QR CODES AND LINKS TO THIRD-PARTY CONTENT
You may gain access to certain third-party content ("Third-Party Sites") by scanning and using the QR Codes that appear in this publication (the "QR Codes"). We do not operate or control in any respect any information, products, or services on such Third-Party Sites linked to by us via the QR Codes included in this publication, and we assume no responsibility for any materials you may access using the QR Codes. Your use of the QR Codes may be subject to terms, limitations, or restrictions set forth in the applicable terms of use or otherwise established by the owners of the Third-Party Sites. Our linking to such Third-Party Sites via the QR Codes does not imply an endorsement or sponsorship of such Third-Party Sites or the information, products, or services offered on or through the Third-Party Sites, nor does it imply an endorsement or sponsorship of this publication by the owners of such Third-Party Sites.

Publisher's Note: Websites listed in this book were active at the time of publication. The publisher is not responsible for websites that have changed their address or discontinued operation since the date of publication. The publisher reviews and updates the websites each time the book is reprinted.

CONTENTS

KEY ICONS TO LOOK FOR:

Words to understand: These words with their easy-to-understand definitions will increase the reader's understanding of the text while building vocabulary skills.

Sidebars: This boxed material within the main text allows readers to build knowledge, gain insights, explore possibilities, and broaden their perspectives by weaving together additional information to provide realistic and holistic perspectives.

Educational videos: Readers can view videos by scanning our QR codes, providing them with additional educational content to supplement the text. Examples include news coverage, moments in history, speeches, iconic sports moments, and much more!

Text-dependent questions: These questions send the reader back to the text for more careful attention to the evidence presented there.

Research projects: Readers are pointed toward areas of further inquiry connected to each chapter. Suggestions are provided for projects that encourage deeper research and analysis.

Series glossary of key terms: This back-of-the-book glossary contains terminology used throughout the series. Words found here increase the reader's ability to read and comprehend higher-level books and articles in this field.

Marine iguanas—lizard-like reptiles of the Galápagos Islands—were some of the strange creatures Darwin encountered on his travels with the Beagle. Their strangeness caused him to start thinking about the origins of these creatures.

WORDS TO UNDERSTAND

brig—a two-masted sailing ship. The *Beagle* was adapted to carry a third mast.

the Creation—God's act of bringing the universe into being.

evolution—gradual change in the characteristics of animals or plants over successive generations.

fossil—the remains, impression or trace of plants or animals, contained in rock.

geology—the scientific study of the origin, history, structure and composition of the earth.

lava—rock that has flowed in liquid form from a volcano.

naturalist—someone who studies plants and animals.

natural selection—the theory whereby those animals and plants best suited to their environment survive, in turn producing correspondingly adapted offspring.

species—a group of animals or plants that is alike in certain ways.

theology—the study of religion.

CHAPTER 1

A Theory that Changed the World

In September 1835, H.M.S. *Beagle*, a tiny survey **brig** of the Royal Navy, dropped anchor off one of the volcanic islands of the Galápagos group, on the northwestern seaboard of South America. On board was a young **naturalist** named Charles Darwin, twenty-six years old and already in the fourth year of a long voyage—one that had so far taken him around South America, and would shortly carry him around the world and back to his home in England.

Darwin's naval shipmates were not impressed with the hot, dusty Galápagos Islands; their job was to make a map of them, and this they did during the next month. But for Darwin himself it was a month of fabulous interest. The islands were like a zoo, with new and different groups of plants and animals—cactuses, shrubs, tortoises, lizards, birds, and insects—waiting for him whenever he went ashore. What he learned on the Galápagos Islands changed the course of his life, for there he discovered the source of a biological theory about the origins of plants and animals that would bring him fame in his own lifetime, and world renown long after his death.

Charles Darwin died in 1882. For the last twenty years or more of his life, he had lived quietly at his home in Kent, England, by then a shy, bewhiskered invalid who pottered in his garden, studying and writing books about earthworms and orchids. He had a loving family, but few

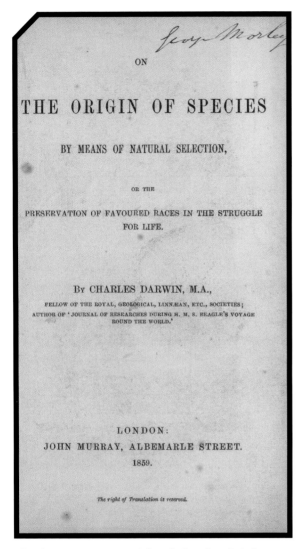

ON

THE ORIGIN OF SPECIES

BY MEANS OF NATURAL SELECTION,

OR THE

PRESERVATION OF FAVOURED RACES IN THE STRUGGLE
FOR LIFE.

By CHARLES DARWIN, M.A.,

FELLOW OF THE ROYAL, GEOLOGICAL, LINNÆAN, ETC., SOCIETIES;
AUTHOR OF 'JOURNAL OF RESEARCHES DURING H. M. S. BEAGLE'S VOYAGE
ROUND THE WORLD.'

LONDON:
JOHN MURRAY, ALBEMARLE STREET.
1859.

The right of Translation is reserved.

Charles Darwin's 1859 book On the Origin of Species *forever changed the way in which people view the world.*

of his old friends were left; he seldom visited London or attended scientific meetings. Darwin had never been a great teacher, or a talented research worker with students about him: in no way was he a brilliant man.

But his research, especially the thinking and writing of his first fifty years, shook Victorian England and made his name renowned throughout Europe and North America. He was respected by many scientists and hated by others, and his theory is as lively and controversial today as it was in his own lifetime. What was so special about Charles Darwin and his theory on the origins of **species**?

Darwin's theory of biological **evolution** tries to explain how and why there are so many kinds (or species) of plants and animals in the world. It suggests that they originated from different ancestral species that lived in the past and are now extinct. Each modern species has evolved—changed over thousands or millions of years from its ancestral form—by a process of selection

For a short video on the age of the Earth, scan here:

and elimination. It is the selected species that are alive today. His theory includes man as a close relation of the apes and monkeys, and indicates that we too evolved, by the same process of **natural selection**, over hundreds of generations, from ape-like ancestors.

We are quite used to evolution today: most people accept it without question. But in Darwin's own day, his revolutionary theories brought a storm of protest, for other beliefs were deeply rooted in the minds of many people. The idea that animals might have evolved, however, was not really new. Darwin's own grandfather Erasmus, a well-known physician and philosopher of the eighteenth century, was writing and talking about evolution long before Charles was born, and Erasmus Darwin was by no means the first to do so. But the idea of evolution offended many people who held other beliefs. Many, for example, took the Bible as literal truth and believed that plants and animals were formed during the six days of **Creation** at the beginning of the world, and had not changed since. They believed too that man was created in God's own image, and to say that he was descended from apes was worse than nonsense—it was blasphemy.

Darwin's theory was not only that plants and animals had evolved, although

Erasmus Darwin was an eighteenth-century physician and philosopher. He was Charles Darwin's grandfather. Erasmus too had been interested in evolution and had developed his own theories on the origin of species long before Charles's birth.

he produced far more evidence—good, solid factual evidence in its favor—than anyone else before or since. His theory was more precise and more exciting than that: it showed how evolution had actually worked and how the processes of natural selection were still working to produce new species every day. People who were opposed to evolution, who had been able to write off Erasmus Darwin's ideas as moonshine, had to take Charles Darwin's carefully thought-out arguments far more seriously.

And they were arguments with frightening implications. If Darwin was right, it followed that man was a product of nature and not a special creation of God. It could follow that natural selection was still working, and that man might one day be eliminated too. Perhaps the whole universe was

USSHER'S CHRONOLOGY

Over the centuries, Christians developed various systems in an attempt to date Biblical events. One of the most ambitious of these was *Annales veteris testamenti, a prima mundi origine deducti* ("Annals of the Old Testament, deduced from the first origins of the world"), a history created by the Anglican archbishop of Ireland, the Reverend James Ussher, in 1650. Ussher used genealogies of Adam, Noah, Abraham, and other legendary figures mentioned in the Bible, along with other dates given in the scriptures, to determine that the world had been created in 4004 BCE, and that the Great Flood had occurred in 2348 BCE. He dated the events of Exodus, when Moses led the Hebrews out of slavery in Egypt, to 1491 BCE. Ussher's chronology, giving a date of about 4,000 years before the birth of Jesus, was in line with other Biblical chronologies of the time.

By the mid-eighteenth century, greater scientific understanding of minerals and geological strata caused some people to question the governed by natural selection, with no divine guiding hand at the tiller. This was discomforting indeed to those who were brought up to believe very deeply that a benevolent God looks after us, and controls everything for the benefit of his special creature—man. Many scientists and thinkers of his time thought Darwin was wrong, just as some still do today. And many more hoped he was wrong, because he upset the beliefs that gave them comfort, in a world that could only too readily seem hostile to puny man.

So the young Charles Darwin of the Galápagos Islands, and the bearded scientist he later became, had a lot to answer for. What sort of a man was he, and how did he come by his theory that so shook the scientific world?

idea that the Earth was less than 6,000 years old. During the 1780s, the Scottish naturalist James Hutton proposed that many of Earth's rock formations had been created through volcanic activity over millions of years, rather than being shaped by the Great Flood as Ussher and others had proposed. During the nineteenth century, Charles Lyell, a geologist who was also a close friend of Charles Darwin, would help Hutton's ideas become accepted by the mainstream.

The changing views about the age of the Earth were very important for the concept of evolution. The changes in species that Darwin theorized could only occur over a long timeline of thousands or millions of years. But while some Bible scholars agreed that the extensive genealogies listed in Genesis could not be used to determine the age of the Earth, they continued trying to date various Biblical events, linking them to archaeological discoveries in Egypt, Palestine, and Persia during the nineteenth and twentieth centuries.

Early Years

Charles Darwin was born in 1809, in the town of Shrewsbury, Shropshire county, England, the fourth child of Robert Darwin, a prosperous doctor with a flourishing practice. His mother Susannah, who died while he was still young, was a daughter of Josiah Wedgwood, owner of the famous pottery. In later life Charles remembered little of her, but enjoyed the company of his Wedgwood cousins, who lived not far away. Doctor Darwin was a huge man who stood over six feet tall and weighed over 300 pounds. Long after he died, Charles spoke fondly of his father as the largest man he ever saw, and the kindest he ever knew. Charles never met his famous grandfather Erasmus, who had died seven years before he was born. But he heard a great deal about him from his father, the practically minded doctor who did not think highly of Erasmus's flights of fancy and philosophical nonsense.

Charles was a quiet boy, and it was intended that he would become a doctor like his father and grandfather before him. He remained at home until he was nine, having a little schooling from his elder sister Caroline, and accompanying Doctor

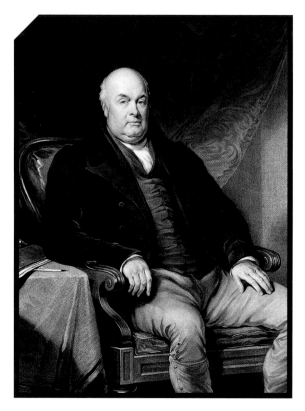

Charles's father, Robert Waring Darwin (1766–1848), was a physician in Shrewsbury. Charles Darwin wrote in later life that Doctor Darwin was the largest man he ever saw, and the kindest man he ever knew.

Charles Robert Darwin (left) and his sister Emily Catherine Darwin, who was a year younger. When Charles was eight years old, his mother died. Young Charles began his formal education a year later.

View of the grammar school in Shrewsbury, England, where Charles Darwin's education began in 1818.

Darwin from time to time on his medical rounds. In his spare time he became a collector—of insects, shells, coins, or anything else that caught his fancy—a hobby that none of his brothers or sisters shared. At the age of nine he was sent to nearby Shrewsbury School, where he lived as a boarder. But as school was only about a mile from his home, he often walked over to visit his family in the evening before lock-up.

He was no scholar: at school he learned Latin and Greek (which bored him) and very little else. This limited curriculum was not unusual for the times, but it did little to stimulate Charles's interests or natural abilities. However, he was a voracious reader with a taste for natural history, travel and poetry. During his schooldays he kept up his interest in collecting, and began to watch closely the birds, butterflies, moths and other creatures that he saw about him.

At sixteen his father took young Charles away from school and enrolled him as a medical student at Edinburgh University. Here his lack of good schooling put him at great disadvantage: he hated the lectures, did not know how to study, and soon found the course dull. He attended lectures in **geology** and found them boring too, although he developed a natural interest in rocks and **fossils** when he was at home in Shrewsbury, and on vacations. Two years at Edinburgh were enough for him: he eventually persuaded his father that he would never make a doctor, and returned home to see what other career he might pursue instead.

Beyond medicine, and excluding the army or navy (in which he had no interest), there was little that a gentleman's son could do in those days

The medical college at Edinburgh University, as it appeared when Charles Darwin was a student there in the 1820s.

except become a clergyman. So Charles Darwin, aged nineteen, joined Christ's College, Cambridge, England, in 1828 as a student of **theology**. It was not a demanding course, and he was able to get by with very little work. Theological studies came easily to him; he "did not then in the least doubt the strict and literal truth of every word of the Bible," on which his divinity course was based. However, he was still far from being a scholar, and spent much of his time at Cambridge in activities not very well suited to a clergyman: he enjoyed hunting, shooting and roaring out songs with lively companions, and going for long rambling walks with geologists and botanists.

In particular he was befriended by Professor John Henslow, a botanist with wide interests in chemistry, minerals and animals, who found the young theology student good company on his daily walks. From Henslow Darwin

Christ's College, Cambridge, where Darwin studied theology. He considered his time there to be wasted, but his friendship with two professors, biologist John Henslow and geologist Adam Sedgewick, started him on his later chosen path.

This detail from a painting by Michelangelo on the ceiling of the Sistine Chapel in Rome, depicts God creating Adam, the first man. In the nineteenth century, most Christians believed that God had created the Earth and everything in it, including humans, in six days, as described in the Biblical book of Genesis.

learned far more about field science—what to look out for, how to observe and record useful detail—than any course of lectures could have taught him. From others at Cambridge, especially Professor Adam Sedgewick, the geologist, he picked up a useful training in field geology—identifying rocks and minerals, working out the rock formations that underlie different landscapes, and finding and recognizing fossils.

All this was incidental to his theological studies, and far, far more interesting to him. At the end of three years, he passed his divinity examinations—just—and obtained his degree, but it was clear both to Darwin, and to his tutors and scientific companions, that he would never become a clergyman. With the interests of a naturalist and the training—

however informal—of a field scientist, he was far better equipped to travel and explore the world than to stay at home as a country parson.

So at the age of twenty-two, Charles Darwin came down from Cambridge with a pass degree—rather a poor one—in theology. Tall, active, strongly built, with reddish hair and a broad, intelligent face, he was very much an outdoor man, with a restless, inquiring mind. He showed not the slightest inclination for further study, unless it involved him in travel and fieldwork, either in Britain or abroad. He had a small personal income and did not need to work for a living, but he had no intention of settling down just yet.

Darwin's Education

What did he know? He had a good grounding in theology and Bible study, and as yet no disagreement with anything he had read in the Bible. He would still, for example, have seen no reason to doubt the Biblical accounts of the Creation and the Flood, and probably tried to interpret his geology in Biblical terms. Many geologists of his time believed that fossils were animals that had died in the Flood, or in several floods and other catastrophes that God from time to time had visited upon the Earth. He may well have accepted, as orthodox churchmen accepted, that the world had been created less than 6,000 years before. During the seventeenth century an Irish theologian, Archbishop James Ussher, had worked out that the Creation occurred in 4004 BCE, specifying even the date and time of day that God had created the world. Ussher's conclusion was based on careful reading of the Scriptures, and Darwin at this stage would probably have seen no reason to doubt it.

Darwin had a basic knowledge of Latin, Greek, algebra and geometry, and some knowledge of chemistry, physics, biology and geology, though certainly far less than that of an average college student today. As a well-read scientist, he would certainly have come across arguments for and against evolution, including his own grandfather's curious books, written in verse. But these were mere philosophical speculations—ideas without evidence to back them up—and of no more than passing interest to a young man with a practical turn of mind, who was discovering the value of facts and the joy of arranging them to discover truths.

What he needed most of all was a change of scenery—a look at other parts of the world that he had read about in traveler's tales. Fired by enthusiasm for travel, he decided on a voyage to Tenerife, in the Canary Islands. The famous German traveler Alexander von Humboldt had been there and found it an exciting island—dominated by a recent volcano and crisscrossed by fields of **lava**. Darwin looked for a passage for himself and even learned a little Spanish, to help him find his way about once he got there. But something far more important came up to change his mind. It was a letter from John Henslow, his old friend at Cambridge, and it was this letter that set him on the much longer voyage that took him to South America, the Galápagos Islands, and around the world to lasting fame.

 TEXT-DEPENDENT QUESTIONS

1. Why did the *Beagle* visit the Galápagos Islands?
2. What is evolution?
3. What Bible-based theory did most people believe in during the nineteenth century?

 RESEARCH PROJECT

Using your school library or the internet, find out what education was like in nineteenth-century Great Britain. Write a two-page paper and share it with your class.

An illustration of H.M.S. Beagle sailing along the coast of South America, from a book about the voyages written by the ship's captain, Robert FitzRoy. Beagle was a small ship, only 90 feet long. Darwin wrote that the vessel rolled uncomfortably even in calm seas and was horribly overcrowded.

WORDS TO UNDERSTAND

fumarole—a natural chimney for gases in the side of a volcano.

pumice—lightweight lava that has poured or blown from a volcano.

secrete—to produce a substance from glands.

CHAPTER 2

The Beagle Adventure

During the eighteenth and nineteenth centuries, the British Royal Navy, apart from its role as a fighting force, took on an important task in between wars—that of surveying coasts and harbors all over the world. The results of its survey missions were accurate charts that provided details of islands and shores, bays, headlands, soundings, reefs, safe channels, anchorages, and harbors, for the use of sailors from every nation. It was a never-ending task because shores are constantly changing. It was also a very important enterprise, because the safety of ships and their crews depends upon accurate, up-to-date charts.

Marine surveys were was traditionally carried out from small, adaptable ships that could work close inshore and enter shallow rivers and creeks in safety. One such ship was H.M.S. *Beagle*, a ten-gun brig. Only 90 feet (28 meters) long, *Beagle* was stoutly built and ideal for her task, though it was small and cramped. With eight officers and a crew of over fifty seamen and Royal marines, there was little room and less comfort in the crowded quarters belowdecks.

Beagle had already seen many years of service as a survey ship. In the summer of 1831 (the year that Charles Darwin left Cambridge), she was lying once again in Plymouth Dockyard, being repaired and refitted for another long survey voyage. Her commanding officer, Captain Robert FitzRoy, was under orders to sail for South America to complete a coastal survey in which both he and *Beagle* had previously been involved. The voyage would probably take four to five years. Captain

Portrait made in 1835 of Captain Robert FitzRoy, the young, intensely religious naval officer who commanded Beagle. FitzRoy argued—and occasionally quarreled—with Darwin over his findings, stimulating Darwin's thinking throughout the long voyage.

FitzRoy, a lively minded young man of twenty-six, with wide interests in science, philosophy and religion, wanted a naturalist on board—someone with scientific training who would collect specimens and write scientific accounts of the places visited.

This was not unusual; in fact, it was part of naval tradition. Many first-rate museum collections, scientific reports, and travel books of the previous century had arisen from naval voyages of exploration and survey. Captain FitzRoy hoped that his surveys of South America, then a relatively unexplored country, would prove just as interesting as the earlier voyages of discovery commanded by George Anson, James Cook, and many others, and bring further credit to the Royal Navy's record of scientific exploration.

But FitzRoy had another objective, also. Deeply religious, he hoped that the naturalist would find evidence to support Biblical accounts of the origins of the world and its early events—the Creation of animals, for example, and the Flood. These must have left their mark somewhere on Earth, he believed, and perhaps a record of them would be found in the uncharted wilds of South America. Their discovery would be an event of both scientific and religious importance.

Darwin Joins the Crew

FitzRoy asked the Navy to find him a suitable naturalist. The request was passed to Cambridge University, where it came into the hands of Professor John Henslow. Henslow was at first tempted to apply for the post himself, but decided against it. Instead he wrote to Charles Darwin, the student of theology, recently graduated, who had accompanied him on his rambles in the Cambridgeshire countryside. Would Darwin be interested in a long voyage to South America and around the world, as an unpaid naturalist aboard H.M.S. *Beagle*?

Darwin received the letter in late August on his return from a geological excursion to North Wales in the company of Adam Sedgewick. All his instincts told him to apply; this was the chance he needed to see the world and, perhaps, establish himself as a scientist. But living at home with his family, he was still very much under the influence of his father, the formidable Doctor Darwin, who counseled strongly against it.

John Henslow, professor of botany at Cambridge, recommended that Darwin join the Beagle voyage. Although Henslow was never one of Darwin's formal teachers at Cambridge, he gave Darwin many useful insights into natural history.

Darwin's uncle Josiah Wedgwood II (1769–1843) ran the pottery firm that his father had started, and also served in Parliament. He encouraged his nephew to seize the opportunity to join the Beagle voyage.

A waste of time, said Doctor Darwin flatly. Having frittered away his chances both at school and at medical college, Charles should now be preparing to enter the Church—not gallivanting off on a wild goose chase with the Navy. Darwin respected his father and saw the force of his argument. Reluctantly he wrote to Henslow, declining the offer.

There the matter might have rested but for Darwin's uncle, Josiah Wedgwood, the son of the famous pottery manufacturer and brother-in-law to Doctor Darwin. "Uncle Jos" was a shrewd businessman and head of the cheerful family of cousins who provided a second home for Darwin at Maer, a few miles from Shrewsbury. Staying with the Wedgwoods for the start of the shooting season early in September, Charles mentioned the offer to his uncle. Josiah was in no doubt: this was an opportunity that must not be missed. Within hours they were back in Shrewsbury, Josiah in furious argument with his brother-in-law, and Charles with a mind that—as he later wrote to his sister—swung like a pendulum from one side of the argument to the other.

Josiah's arguments won. Doctor Darwin withdrew his objections, and Charles wrote quickly to Henslow, canceling his earlier letter. Then, the shooting holiday forgotten, he took an express coach to Cambridge for a brief word with Henslow, before setting out for London. There, on September 5, 1831, he met Captain FitzRoy for the first time.

It was a favorable meeting; the two liked each other and got on well together from the start. Darwin saw a responsible young ship's captain—lofty, authoritarian, and used to giving orders, but also friendly, approachable, and acutely intelligent. Everyone thought and spoke highly of FitzRoy. FitzRoy observed a diffident and immature young man, but recognized him as honest, straightforward, likeable, and keen to talk over the prospects for the voyage. Together they traveled to Plymouth (a three-day journey by sea) and Darwin saw the *Beagle*, scruffy and unshipshape in the hands of the dockyard refitters. FitzRoy and Darwin weighed each other up and decided: Darwin would sail with the *Beagle*.

The Voyage Begins

Darwin had a month to collect his gear—boots and clothing for all weathers, books and firearms, bottles and alcohol for preserving specimens, notebooks. Darwin brought everything he would need for a

To see a short video on Captain FitzRoy and Darwin, scan here:

voyage that would last at least two years, and might last five. On board by the sailing date, October 24, he found the *Beagle* still not ready to leave, and spent a miserable, unsettled two months in Plymouth waiting for the refit to be completed. They attempted to set sail in early December, and again just before Christmas, but each time met with contrary winds and had to return to harbor. Finally they left on December 27, 1831, slipping down the channel with easterly winds in their sails, and out into the open Atlantic Ocean.

CHARLES LYELL

The Scottish geologist Charles Lyell (1797–1875) was one of the most important scientists of the nineteenth century. He expanded on the writings of James Hutton, another Scottish geologist, who had proposed in the eighteenth century that the Earth was far older than most people could imagine. Lyell's first book, *Principles of Geology*, was published in three volumes between 1830 and 1833. In it, Lyell proposed a theory he called the Doctrine of Uniformity. This was the idea that the same natural laws and processes that operate in the universe now have always operated in the universe in the past and apply everywhere. According to Lyell, the Earth's geological features had been shaped over a long period of time by natural processes like volcanic activity and erosion.

Lyell had asked Captain Robert FitzRoy to search for unusual rock formations during the *Beagle* voyage, and FitzRoy gave Darwin the first volume of *Principles of Geology* at the start of the voyage in 1831. During the voyage Darwin gathered information about geological formations that supported Lyell's theories. When the *Beagle* returned

At her best in sheltered coastal waters, H.M.S. *Beagle* was a thoroughly uncomfortable ship at sea. Rolling and tossing in the rough waters of the Atlantic in the depths of winter, Charles Darwin for the first time succumbed to seasickness, an illness that would plague him continuously all the time he was at sea. Brought on by the motion of the ship, seasickness affects some people for just the first few days at sea; others never get used to it, particularly on small ships, and Darwin was one of those.

in 1836, the two men met and became close friends.

Charles Lyell was also known for his studies of earthquakes and volcanic activity, as well as the formation of rock layers, both sedimentary and volcanic. Darwin discussed his ideas about natural selection with Lyell as early as 1842. However, Lyell was a devout Christian and personally doubted the theory of evolution. He did, however, help to arrange publication of papers explaining the theory by Darwin and Alfred Russel Wallace in 1858, despite his religious reservations.

Sir Charles Lyell

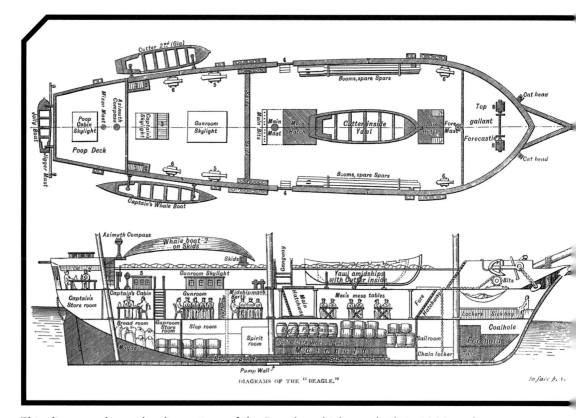

This diagram shows the dimensions of the Beagle, which was built in 1820 and made its first survey voyage from 1826 to 1830. When the ship's captain died on this journey, Robert Fitzroy was promoted to command of the Beagle.

Seasickness is not just a matter of feeling sick; every movement brings giddiness and nausea, and a strange feeling of weariness and depression. "The misery I endured from seasickness is far beyond what I ever guessed at," he wrote during the early days of the voyage. Cold and wet, cramped in the tiny stern cabin that he shared with FitzRoy, he could neither read, write, nor even think properly as the ship rolled and heaved its way across a storm-lashed Bay of Biscay.

The first port-of-call, Tenerife in the Canary Islands, was a great disappointment; there was a fear of the Plague and nobody was allowed ashore. Things were better when they stopped for three weeks at the Cape Verde Islands, a volcanic group further south in the Atlantic Ocean. In the calmer sub-tropical seas, Darwin had been able to read some chapters of an important new book—Charles Lyell's *Principles of Geology*—given to him just before he left England. Now he was seeing firsthand a kind of landscape described by Lyell, but never known to the author on his English excursions—the lava flows, ashcones, **pumice**, and **fumaroles** of volcanic islands, relatively recent in formation and uncluttered by vegetation.

He saw, and wondered at, lava that had covered a bed of marine shells and was now halfway up a cliff face high above sea level. Had the sea sunk or the land risen? Darwin missed very little and his scientific log grew daily, filled with items carefully and clearly noted down. At first uncertain of his abilities, he wondered in an early letter to Henslow if he was noting "the right facts, the important facts." As time went on, both log and letters reflected his growing self-confidence. He recorded everything he saw, and he missed few opportunities for seeing and visiting interesting places.

On St. Paul's Rocks, a tiny patch of mid-oceanic reefs between Africa and South America, Darwin noted two kinds of seabirds, and a strange mixture of small animals living among them—parasitic flies and ticks, moths, beetles, woodlice and spiders. In Bahia, the *Beagle*'s first South American landfall, he noted with delight the richness of the tropical forest—the huge trees, the variety of birds, the brilliance of the flowers and butterflies. He noted the continuous noise of insects that could be heard from a ship anchored some way offshore, and the silence within the forest during the heat of the day. Caught in a heavy tropical downpour, he noted the torrents of water running down the tree trunks. Back on board he recorded with amusement the habits of the puffer fish, which blows itself up like a spiny ball when alarmed and **secretes** a beautiful red fluid from the skin of the abdomen.

At sea again, sailing south through calmer coastal waters, he noted patches of discoloration on the surface of the ocean. Trailing fine homemade nets, he filtered out the tiny plants and brilliantly colored animals that caused the

An extinct crater and basalt shoreline on Sao Vicente Island in the Cape Verde archipelago.

patches, examining and identifying them under his primitive microscope. On a similar investigation off the Canary Islands, he had marveled that creatures "so low in the scale of Nature, are most exquisite in their forms and rich colors," and wondered why "so much beauty should be apparently created for such little purpose." Now he was asking questions more scientific and practical: Where were these huge concentrations of drifting plants and animals coming from? And why did they form lines in the water? The theologian in Darwin was disappearing and the down-to-earth scientist was emerging, as H.M.S. *Beagle* rolled her way south along the coast of South America.

TEXT-DEPENDENT QUESTIONS

1. Who recommended Darwin for the naturalist position on the *Beagle*?
2. What illness did Darwin suffer from during the *Beagle*'s voyage?
3. What was the *Beagle*'s first South American landfall?

 ## RESEARCH PROJECT

The *Beagle* was one of more than 100 small ships built for the British Royal Navy between 1807 and 1826. The ships all used the same design, and were known as the Cherokee class, named after H.M.S. *Cherokee*, the first ship that used this design. Find out more about how the Navy used these ships, and report your findings to the class.

This portrait of Charles Darwin was made during the late 1830s, after the Beagle returned to England.

CHAPTER 3

South America

April 1832 found Charles Darwin in Rio de Janeiro, living ashore for three months while H.M.S. *Beagle* completed local survey work along the coast of Brazil. Lodging in a cottage outside the town with Augustus Earle, the expedition artist, and Midshipman King, he wandered in the tropical forest that began at his doorstep, collecting beetles, spiders, worms, butterflies, parrots, monkeys—everything that came his way. He found some English-speaking settlers in the town, and traveled with them to their estates inland, riding for ten hours a day on horseback and resting overnight in flea-ridden inns.

The Brazilian rainforest astonished Darwin, not only with whole groups of plants and animals that he had never seen before, but with the immense variety of species to be found in every corner of it, at every level from treetops to the ground. There was nothing in the temperate forests back home in England that could match this tropical richness. Bewildered at first by its luxuriance, it took him some time to understand and enjoy it.

Staying ashore gave Darwin time for leisure. Now, no longer a mere collector in a hurry, he was able to watch the animals going about their daily lives in the forest—something that very few naturalists before him had been able to do. He watched wasps and hummingbirds searching for their favorite foods, noted how soldier ants made paths on the forest floor, how spiders hunted, how butterflies drummed their wings in courtship flight. He investigated fireflies and glowworms to see how they produced their flickering lights, and jumping beetles to find out how they jumped. It was a period of concentrated self-education, from which he emerged with bulging notebooks and a whole new concept of animals' lives. A thousand different species of animals can live together in the forest because they are adapted in a thousand different ways, he realized, with each playing a different role in the life of the forest community.

The Voyage Continues

In July 1832 Darwin re-embarked on the *Beagle* and headed south for Montevideo. Here, to his surprise, the former theology student found himself marching down the main street with cutlass in hand and pistols in

Modern-day gauchos (South American cowboys) round up a herd of cattle on the pampas of Uruguay. During the Beagle voyage, Darwin traveled for many miles over the plains with the gauchos, living rough while he collected specimens and made notes.

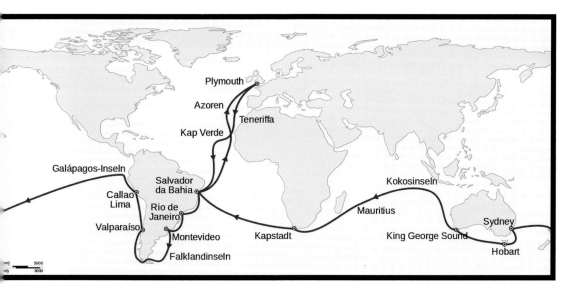

This map shows the route taken by the *Beagle* during its five-year-long voyage of exploration.

belt, as part of a naval landing party helping to quell a riot and protect the property of the British residents. Back aboard the *Beagle*, Darwin and his shipmates sailed south to Patagonia and he continued with his biological work.

While the *Beagle* sailed back and forth offshore in her seemingly endless survey of the coast, Darwin made many excursions inland, across the dry, dreary grasslands and plains—a way of life that was to occupy him for the next two years.

Late July found him in southern Patagonia, examining flamingos, crabs, and worms living in pools of concentrated brine surrounded by miles of desert sands. "Well may we affirm," he wrote, "that every part of the world is habitable! Whether lakes of brine, or those subterranean ones hidden beneath volcanic mountains—warm mineral springs—the wide expanse and depths of the ocean—the upper reaches of the atmosphere, and even the surface of perpetual snow—all support organic beings." Traveling again on horseback, he crossed the desert plains with a party of **gauchos**,

Lion marmosets were among the intriguing monkeys that Charles Darwin encountered in the rainforests of South America. He studied everything he saw, and collected specimens to send back to Cambridge.

stayed overnight with an old soldier of the Spanish Army who had fought with Napoleon in Russia, and scanned the horizon for bands of hostile Indians who would have killed him without question if they had met. This exciting life in distant lands was a far cry from the comfortable, sheltered days of Shrewsbury and Cambridge, and Darwin loved every minute of it.

Caught out one night after sunset and obliged to camp, he killed an armadillo for supper—a small, insect-eating mammal with a hard shell, one of several species that abounded on the plains. Roasted gaucho-style in its shell, it was barely big enough to feed him and his companion. "It

A brilliantly colored hummingbird found in the Brazilian rainforest. With its long tongue, it is perfectly adapted to lick nectar from tropical flowers, hovering near with its tiny wings whirring.

seems almost a pity to kill such nice little animals," wrote Darwin, "for as a gaucho said, while sharpening his knife on the back of one—they are so quiet." Weeks later he was down on the coast, hunting armadillos of another kind—giant fossil armadillos as big as a car, whose bones could be found in the cliffs and beaches near Punto Alta.

Why were the fossil armadillos so enormous, while the modern ones, obviously closely related, were no bigger than cats? By now Darwin was sure that the fossils represented an era long past—a time when

While in South America, Darwin found fossil bones of a now-extinct creature called a Glyptodon; this example is preserved in a museum in Berlin. The Glyptodon resembled the much smaller armadillos that Darwin observed living on the South American plains during the 1830s. Darwin also found the fossil remains of other giant mammals, such as ground sloths (Mylodon), that had lived in the cliffs near Bahia thousands of years ago.

Natives of Tierra del Fuego hail the Beagle *in this painting by an artist on board the ship, Conrad Martens. Darwin was amazed that they lived so poorly, almost without clothes, in a cold and rainy climate. Even their crude shelters let in the rain and snow.*

landscapes, climates, and vegetation were vastly different from those of the present. Where were these big animals at the time of the Flood? Obviously left behind by the Ark, said Captain FitzRoy (with whom Darwin discussed his new ideas when they met briefly in port). But now Darwin suspected that there had been many "floods"—occasions when animals of all kinds had been overwhelmed by disasters and wiped out, to be replaced by others. Had there, then, been several separate creations of species and not just the one mentioned in the Bible? Or were new species perhaps being created continuously? Only a part of the truth was disclosed on the cold plains of southern Argentina—just how important a part, Darwin had yet to learn.

Sailing South

Beagle sailed southward to Tierra del Fuego, a region of cold forests and glaciers at the tip of South America, close to Cape Horn. Here, in December 1832, Darwin met for the first time a primitive human population, almost untouched by civilization. He was impressed by their hardiness—they wore little clothing, despite the intense cold, and slept on the ground with rain pouring through the roofs of their ramshackle huts. They were more like animals than men, thought Darwin. Only later did it occur to him that primitive man might indeed be closer to animals—the animal species from which we have all descended.

Darwin did not much like the Fuegians. They did little to improve their own miserable lot, and had no skills; they could be cannibals when it suited them, they were cruel to each other and constantly demanded knives and blankets from the crew of the *Beagle*. Captain FitzRoy was returning to their homeland three young Fuegians whom he had kidnapped on his previous voyage. They had been educated in England and converted to Christianity, and FitzRoy hoped they would now spread civilization and the Christian message among their own people. Darwin was sure they would not be able to do so, and events proved him right: the three "missionaries" soon

Patagonia, Argentina

Scan here for a video showing the wildlife and terrain of Patagonia:

threw off all traces of education and reverted to their primitive state, much to FitzRoy's dismay.

The *Beagle* then sailed on to the Falkland Islands, where Darwin found little to interest him, and back to the Plata estuary. From late April to July 1833, while the ship continued her survey, Darwin made excursions inland across the plains north of Montevideo, collecting specimens of birds, mammals and reptiles. Traveling with two armed guards to protect him from bandits, he stayed overnight in small settlements, where he mystified the villagers by showing them his pocket compass, and lighting matches with his teeth. Even washing his face in the morning caused much speculation in one village: the local people, who saw no reason to wash themselves, suspected he might be a heretic, and therefore dangerous. Darwin wondered at the absence of trees, the strong smell of the local deer, the size of the **capybaras**, and the many kinds of birds of prey that shared the spoils of the open grasslands.

Taken south again into Patagonia by the *Beagle*, Darwin spent the rest of the year making overland journeys, from the Rio Negro to Bahia Blanca, and then crossing the **pampas** to Buenos Aires and on to Santa Fé on the Parana River. These explorations convinced him that virtually the whole southern end of South America had once been sea bed, raised by some vast force to form salty, windswept plains. FitzRoy would have none of it; for him the Biblical account of the Flood explained everything, and their arguments grew more bitter and impatient each time they met.

With the Patagonian survey finished, the *Beagle* sailed south again, passing through the straits of Tierra del Fuego in winter and heading north to Valparaiso on the west coast of South America. For over a year, from July 1834 to September 1835, the west coast was surveyed. FitzRoy was now ill from overwork and anxiety; there were repeated quarrels, and Darwin spent as much time as he could ashore. His next excursion, lasting six weeks, took him up into the Andes behind Valparaiso. For the first time he saw high mountain plants and animals, and again his notebooks were filled with sketches, comments, and speculations.

The geology of the Andes intrigued him even more than the plant and animal life. At a height of 12,000 feet (3,700 meters)—too high to boil the potatoes properly, he noted—there were beds of seashells. Lower down there was a forest of fossil pines surrounded by marine deposits. Both these finds convinced him that the rocks of the Andes once formed the sea bed, and had been thrust upward by unimaginable forces. Later, far south along the coast of Chile, he witnessed these forces in action—first a volcanic eruption, then an earthquake that shattered the town of Concepción and the neighboring port of Talcahuano.

Beagle sailed into Talcahuano a few days after the earthquake, and Darwin and FitzRoy rode inland to Concepción. To FitzRoy, the earthquake was a visitation from God—a punishment for the wickedness of the people. Darwin did not argue; he quietly noted details of the catastrophe—which buildings had fallen, which walls of the cathedral had split, exactly how long it had taken for the tidal wave that followed the earthquake to hit the town, and above all, how high the shore had risen (a matter of several feet in places) as a result of just one moderately severe earthquake. No longer could he believe in the permanence of mountains. "Nothing," he wrote, "not even the wind that blows, is so unstable as the level of the crust of the earth."

With the *Beagle* now working the west coast from southern Chile to Peru, Darwin continued his inland journeys, exploring the Andes and the coastal plains at their foot. Riding hard and living rough on his excursions, he began to look forward to his short stays aboard the *Beagle*, where he could be sure of clean clothes, reasonable meals, and the cheerful company of his shipmates. To them he was a sort of mascot—some called him "Philosopher," others "Flycatcher"—and all respected him for his hard work, good humor, and physical toughness. FitzRoy, now recovered, was better company and ready for a friendly argument again.

Darwin enjoyed good health while he was ashore, apart from bouts of fever and other minor ailments. But travel in the Andes held a hidden danger, one that may have affected his future health permanently. He

Inland from Valparaiso, Darwin climbed into in the Andes. Finding fossil shells among the high peaks, he concluded that the rocks had formed a long time ago on the bed of the ocean, and had been forced up by earth movements.

was bitten by an insect called the Benchuga bug which, like flies and mosquitoes, feeds on the blood of warm-blooded animals. The bug is now known to carry Chagas' disease, a kind of sleeping sickness. He kept one of these bugs in a box, to study at leisure, allowing it to bite him several times. There were no immediate ill effects, but the prolonged illness he suffered on his return to England may well have originated from his too-close inquiry into the habits of the Benchuga bug.

TEXT-DEPENDENT QUESTIONS

1. What did Darwin encounter in Tierra del Fuego?
2. When did the *Beagle* crew survey the west coast of South America?
3. What event witnessed by Darwin made him question the permanence of mountains and other geological features?

RESEARCH PROJECT

Using the internet or your school library, do some research into British expeditions to survey and chart the world's oceans during the nineteenth century. What were the reasons for these expeditions? What were the benefits to the British government and military, or to the public at large? Write a two-page report with your findings and share it with your class.

Among the puzzling creatures of the Galápagos Islands were the giant tortoises, weighing far more than a man. Each island in the group had its own slightly different stocks of tortoises, with distinctive shells. This specimen is found on the island of Santa Cruz.

 WORDS TO UNDERSTAND

aboriginal—native of a country, living there before the arrival of explorers or colonists.

atolls—ring-shaped coral reefs enclosing a lagoon.

barnacle—a shelled animal (crustacean) that lives attached to rocks, ships' timbers etc.

finch—a small seed-eating bird.

CHAPTER 4

The Galápagos Islands and Home

H.M.S. *Beagle* left Callao, her final port in South America, on September 7, 1835, and dropped anchor off Chatham Island, in the Galápagos group, just over a week later. The next five weeks were some of Darwin's busiest during the *Beagle* voyage. He visited many islands, and camped for a week on James Island, in the middle of the group, with the ship's surgeon and three crew members for company.

Darwin as usual collected specimens and recorded his impressions. There were strange animals to be seen—giant tortoises, land iguanas like huge lizards, and even larger marine iguanas that swam in the sea, basked on the rocks, and ate seaweed. And there were more familiar creatures— doves, **finches**, owls, hawks, and many others, all similar to those he had come across in mainland South America. Except that—and the point did not strike him fully until he was examining his specimens later—they were all subtly different from the mainland forms, and different too in each of the various islands of the Galápagos group. Most of the animals and over half the flowering plants were species found only on the Galápagos. Of seventy-one species of plants collected on James Island, thirty-eight—just over half—were unknown outside the Galápagos, and only eight could be found on other islands within the group.

"I never dreamed," he wrote, "that islands, about fifty or sixty miles apart, and most of them in sight of each other … would have been differently tenanted…. It is the fate of most voyagers, no sooner to discover what is most interesting in any locality, than they are hurried from it; but I ought, perhaps, to be thankful that I obtained sufficient material to establish this most remarkable fact." And remarkable it was. As Darwin pointed out later, it would have been less surprising if the islands had contained completely different sets of plants and animals; for them to have similar but not identical ones was puzzling indeed. He noted strong sea currents flowing between the islands and lack of winds. These factors helped to isolate the

THE GALÁPAGOS ISLANDS

The Galápagos Islands is the name for an archipelago located approximately 600 miles (966 km) off the coast of Ecuador, South America. The archipelago includes fifteen large islands and hundreds of small islands, covering an area of 12,798 square miles (33,134 sq km). The islands were formed by the eruption of volcanoes that are now extinct, and are composed mainly of a type of rock called "basalt."

The Galápagos region is an amazing place. There are about 10,000 people living on the Galápagos Islands, but the islands' most famous residents are plants and animals. There are over 5,000 species living on the Galápagos Islands. The islands are one of the most biologically diverse areas in the world. According to scientists, more than 1,900 species are found nowhere else. This is because the islands are so isolated. Over time, the plants and animals there developed characteristics different from those found anywhere else in the world.

Even though the Galápagos Islands are located along the equator, they are not unbearably hot. The average year-round temperature islands from each other and would prevent birds, seeds, and spores being blown between them.

So why were the tortoises different enough for even a casual observer to be able to identify at a glance which island they had come from? Why were the marine iguanas notably bigger on Albemarle Island than anywhere else? Why did each island have its own species of finches, all clearly similar though different in form? Some were small-billed, some large-billed, some even with stout woodpecker bills that they used for digging insects out of

in this region is 85°F (30°C), which is considered subtropical, or just below tropical. This is partly because the temperature of the surrounding waters is often affected by a current from the South Pole known as the Peru, or Humboldt, current. This polar current helps to cool the temperature of the air above the Galápagos Islands. Another reason for the subtropical climate of the Galápagos Islands is ocean upwelling. Upwelling, which refers to the rise of deep water to the surface, is caused by ocean currents and winds. The water rising from the bottom of the ocean is colder than the surface water. In some areas, the water temperature can fall below 68°F (20°C). This water cools the Galápagos Islands' climate, too.

Today the islands are the property of Ecuador, which considers the Galápagos to be a national treasure. Ninety-seven percent of the Galápagos Islands' land area is now a national park. Some of the islands' unique residents include Galápagos fur seals, Galápagos penguins, marine iguanas, pega-pega trees, lava lizards, and Galápagos tortoises.

On the Galápagos Islands Darwin found many plants and animals new to him, though some—like these giant iguanas—were probably related to those on the mainland. Somehow the islands had changed them. Even the marine iguanas of the different islands varied slightly from each other. Although the islands were only a few miles apart—often in sight of each other—the stocks remained separate and were not interbreeding.

the shrubs and cacti. "One is astonished," wrote Darwin, "at the amount of creative force, if such an expression may be used, displayed on these small, barren and rocky islands." But "creative force" was no explanation at all. He continued to puzzle over it long after the Galápagos Islands had disappeared over the *Beagle*'s stern.

The Voyage Home

After leaving the islands, Darwin was on his way home—tired, sated with facts, figures and impressions, loaded with bottled specimens and bulging notebooks. The *Beagle* crossed the Pacific Ocean, calling at Tahiti, New Zealand, and Australia. Darwin, as usual, explored inland at each stop. Although still interested in geology, flora, and fauna, he now paid particular attention to the natives he met, contrasting their old ways of life with those they were now acquiring under the influence of Christian missionaries from Europe. All of the peoples he met seemed superior to the Fuegians in intelligence and enterprise. The Tahitians impressed Darwin with their jolly ways and strong physiques, the New Zealanders with their warlike natures, and the Australian **aboriginals** because of their hunting skills.

Darwin mused on the gradual decline of native populations in countries that Europeans were invading and taking over. Diseases introduced by the settlers were one important cause; even measles could bring death to island populations that had never been exposed to them. But there was something more. "The varieties of man seem to act on each other in the same way as different species of animals—the stronger always extirpating

Scan here to see the unique wildlife of the Galápagos Islands:

Like the tortoises, the finches varied slightly on the different Galápagos Islands. Some species had grown large, with heavy bills for cracking open big seeds, while others were small, with much finer bills. Darwin speculated that they all must have derived from the same few ancestors, evolving their different forms after arriving on the islands thousands of years earlier.

the weaker," he wrote. This theme of competition—rivalry between similar forms, leading to the dominance of one and extinction of the other—would prove to be an important link in the chain of evidence that Darwin was unknowingly collecting for his theory of natural selection.

Beagle continued westward into the Indian Ocean, calling briefly at Keeling Island in April 1836, where Darwin and FitzRoy together studied the structure of coral **atolls**. Each marveled in his own way that islands and reefs many miles across could be formed by myriads of coral polyps, tiny animals no bigger than pinheads. Darwin later developed his observations into a general theory on the structure and distribution of coral reefs—how they form, and how their growth depends on a slow, progressive sinking of the land in relation to sea level.

After visiting Mauritius, the Cape of Good Hope, St. Helena, and Ascension Island, the *Beagle* returned briefly to Bahia, in South America, to complete the circuit of the earth and check Captain FitzRoy's twenty-two chronometers, which were essential for ensuring the accuracy of the survey. They then set course for the North Atlantic and on October 2, 1836, H.M.S. *Beagle* slipped quietly into Falmouth Harbor. Almost five years after he had first stepped aboard the ship, Charles Darwin stepped ashore again in England, and headed north for his home in Shrewsbury.

A coral island in the Pacific Ocean, surrounded by reefs. Darwin was fascinated by the way that fringing reefs formed around underwater volcanic peaks.

Revealing His Discoveries

After a happy reunion with his family—"The shape of his head is quite altered," declared Doctor Darwin approvingly—Charles spent the following weeks in Cambridge and London, where he worked furiously on his collection of specimens and reports. During the next months and years, he edited five volumes of scientific reports, and his *Journal of the Voyage of the Beagle*, published in 1839, established him firmly as a popular writer. In the same year he married his cousin Emma, youngest daughter of Uncle Josiah Wedgwood, and set up home with her on Gower Street, London.

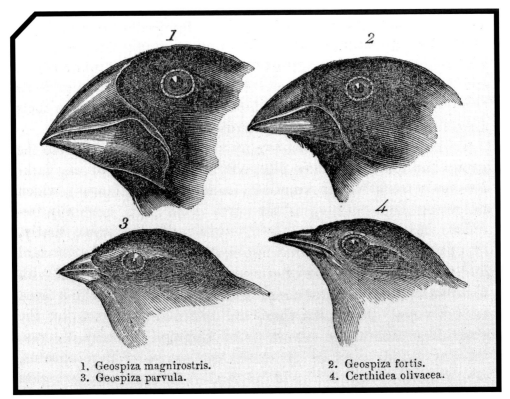

1. Geospiza magnirostris.
2. Geospiza fortis.
3. Geospiza parvula.
4. Certhidea olivacea.

Illustration from Darwin's book Journal of the Voyage of the Beagle *displaying four types of finch that Darwin observed in the Galápagos Islands, showing the differentiation of their bills. The book quickly became a bestseller.*

Appointed secretary of the prestigious Geological Society, he developed a wide circle of scientific friends and acquaintances, and seemed set for a life of activity in the bustling scientific community of London.

However, ill health began to creep up on him. By 1842, London was proving too tiring, and he moved with his growing family to Down House, in the village of Downe, near Sevenoaks in Kent. Soon he gave up traveling to London, settling in to the life of a semi-invalid in the country. After completing his work on the *Beagle* collections, he turned to other subjects for research closer at hand—a study of

In 1839 Charles Darwin married Emma Wedgwood, youngest daughter of his uncle Josiah. It was a happy marriage and they had seven surviving children. This watercolor painting of Emma was made a year after their marriage.

barnacles; breeding domestic cattle, sheep and horses; pigeon fancying; beekeeping; the habits of earthworms; and many other topics that kept his inquiring mind busy. He opened up, too, an extensive correspondence with naturalists all over the world who could help him with his research.

But beneath all this was fermenting his great concept of evolution, "that mystery of mysteries," he liked to call it, "the first appearance of new beings on this earth." Darwin had become convinced that species had evolved, developing over a long period of time from different ancestral forms. Despite the Bible and those who believed its literal truth, Darwin was convinced that the enormous variety of living creatures, past and present, could not be accounted for by a single act of Creation 6,000 years ago.

But how did the process of evolution work? Darwin started his first notebook on the subject in 1837, the year after *Beagle* berthed in Falmouth. Not until twenty-two years later did he finally publish the result of his research. *On the Origin of Species by Means of Natural Selection*, published in 1859, drew together the many strands of ideas that had spun in his mind during the *Beagle* voyage and afterward, and established, beyond doubt, Darwin's reputation as a scientist and original thinker.

TEXT-DEPENDENT QUESTIONS

1. What was notable about the marine iguanas on Albermarle Island in the Galápagos group?
2. What impressed Darwin about the people of Tahiti?
3. When was Darwin's *Journal of the Voyage of the Beagle* published?

 RESEARCH PROJECT

Darwin's thinking on evolution was influenced by a number of scientists who preceeded him, including Georges Cuvier, Pierre Maupertuis, Jean-Baptiste Lamarck, W. C. Wells, J. C. Pritchard, Patrick Matthew, and his own grandfather, Erasmus Darwin. Choose one of these scientists to learn more about. Write a two-page report about your subject's contributions to the field of evolutionary science, and share it with the class.

Down House, in the village of Downe in Kent, where Charles and Emma Darwin lived and raised their children. Darwin seldom left Down House except for very brief visits to London.

WORDS TO UNDERSTAND

embryo—an animal in the early stages of development.

monograph—a paper, book or other writing concerned with a single subject.

organ—the part of an animal or plant that has adapted for a special function.

rudimentary organ—an organ that is imperfectly developed or has lost its original function.

CHAPTER 5

The Origin of Species

Darwin was never anxious to publish his theory. He knew that he would be accused of irreverence and blasphemy once it was published, so he needed to be certain that there was no mistake—that every aspect of his theory was as sound as he could make it. He drew up a first draft in 1842, expanded it in 1844, and then set out to collect the vast weight of evidence that he hoped would make this theory unassailable. For eight years he worked on the biology of barnacles, producing four **monographs** on the subject while the question of evolution remained at the back of his mind. Then, in the late 1850s, he started to write about his theory seriously, planning a major work for publication sometime in the next decade.

But in June 1858 he received a letter from one of his overseas correspondents that altered his plans completely. Alfred Russell Wallace was a professional naturalist and collector, who at that time was working in the East Indies. For some months he too had been considering possible ways in which species might be formed. The answer had come to him while he was a suffering from a bout of high fever: that the natural variation that, within a species, gives animals their individuality, is maintained and in time fixed to produce new strains. This he wrote in a brief paper of a dozen pages and sent to Darwin, asking if it seemed worthy of publication.

Wallace's idea came very close to what Darwin himself had been thinking, although it was little more than a brilliant hunch. Darwin was only mildly dismayed at the possibility of someone else publishing on the subject before he himself was ready to do so. He lost no time in sending

Working independently, Alfred Russel Wallace developed a theory similar to Darwin's.

Wallace's paper to two of his closest friends, both renowned scientists. One was Joseph Dalton Hooker, a distinguished botanist; the other was Charles Lyell, the geologist. Darwin recommended that Wallace's paper should be published as soon as possible. However, recognizing the very thorough work that Darwin had done on the subject, Hooker and Lyell thought it fair that both scientists should be given credit for the idea. So they arranged for papers by both Darwin and Wallace to be read at the next meeting of the Linnean Society, where other London scientists could hear these new views on the origin of species for the first time.

The papers, read on July 1, 1858, caused no stir at all. But Darwin's book, completed hurriedly and published the following year, began a groundswell of controversy and protest that grew with every passing month. Not everyone who read *The Origin of Species* bothered to understand all of its implications, for it was a long book, crammed with examples and closely reasoned argument. Darwin did not set out to provoke a storm or popularize his belief. He wanted only to present his idea, and the weight of evidence supporting it, as clearly and fully as possible.

On the Tendency of Species to form Varieties; and on the Perpetuation of Varieties and Species by Natural Means of Selection. By CHARLES DARWIN, Esq., F.R.S., F.L.S., & F.G.S., and ALFRED WALLACE, Esq. Communicated by Sir CHARLES LYELL, F.R.S., F.L.S., and J. D. HOOKER, Esq., M.D., V.P.R.S., F.L.S., &c.

[Read July 1st, 1858.]

London, June 30th, 1858.

MY DEAR SIR,—The accompanying papers, which we have the honour of communicating to the Linnean Society, and which all relate to the same subject, viz. the Laws which affect the Production of Varieties, Races, and Species, contain the results of the investigations of two indefatigable naturalists, Mr. Charles Darwin and Mr. Alfred Wallace.

These gentlemen having, independently and unknown to one another, conceived the same very ingenious theory to account for the appearance and perpetuation of varieties and of specific forms on our planet, may both fairly claim the merit of being original thinkers in this important line of inquiry; but neither of them having published his views, though Mr. Darwin has for many years past been repeatedly urged by us to do so, and both authors having now unreservedly placed their papers in our hands, we think it would best promote the interests of science that a selection from them should be laid before the Linnean Society.

Taken in the order of their dates, they consist of:—

1. Extracts from a MS. work on Species*, by Mr. Darwin, which was sketched in 1839, and copied in 1844, when the copy was read by Dr. Hooker, and its contents afterwards communicated to Sir Charles Lyell. The first Part is devoted to "The Variation of Organic Beings under Domestication and in their Natural State;" and the second chapter of that Part, from which we propose to read to the Society the extracts referred to, is headed, "On the Variation of Organic Beings in a state of Nature; on the Natural Means of Selection; on the Comparison of Domestic Races and true Species."

2. An abstract of a private letter addressed to Professor Asa Gray, of Boston, U.S. in October 1857, by Mr. Darwin, in which

The first page of the paper published jointly by Darwin and Wallace in June 1858, and read publicly at a meeting of the Linnean Society in London.

The Origin of Species

Darwin based his thinking on two propositions that he believed everyone would agree with. The first was that, within species, plants and animals vary slightly from one individual to another (identical twins are a rare exception), and that at least some of these variations are clearly inheritable. The second was that plants and animals produce many more offspring—seeds, eggs, or young—than can possibly survive; however, as their numbers change little from year to year, there must be a constant struggle for existence, in which for every few survivors, many are lost.

Putting these two propositions together, Darwin thought it likely that, if some of the small points of variation gave advantages—such as slightly longer legs in running animals, better camouflage in hunted species, or shorter ears and thicker fur for those living in cold climates, for example—then animals that lacked those favorable variations would be at a disadvantage in the struggle for survival. Conversely, animals that had these advantages would be more likely to survive, reproduce, and pass on their favorable variations to their offspring.

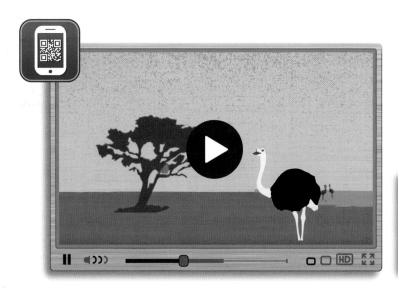

For an analysis of The Origin of Species, *scan here:*

So over the years, animals that became slightly separated from their parent group—perhaps blown out onto an island, or moving a few miles away to a slightly different climate—would gradually accumulate variations that favored them in their new environment. They would begin to look different from each other, and eventually become recognizable as distinct species. This could have happened several times over on the Galápagos Islands, for example, to produce the different species of plants, tortoises, and birds on each island. It would help to explain, too, why plants and animals always seem so well adapted to their

Sir Joseph Dalton Hooker, a distinguished botanist and personal friend of Darwin's, who supported him after the publication of The Origin of Species.

environments. Each organism is the end-product of this selective process—the failures and misfits are constantly being weeded out.

Darwin called this process "natural selection," drawing an analogy from the selection practiced by animal breeders. From each new litter of animals or batch of young plants, the breeder or nurseryman selects individuals with the qualities he wants to perpetuate, and rejects the rest. In this way, over many generations, horses as different as Shetland ponies, hunters, and Percherons; dairy cattle with high milk yields; vigorous wheats, high-yielding

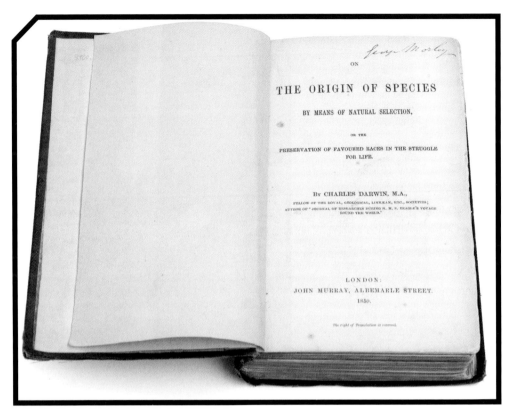

First edition of The Origin of Species, *published in 1859.*

peas and beans, and many beautiful flowering plants from less attractive wild stocks, have been produced. Human selection achieved these differences in a few decades. Natural selection had been operating over millions of years to produce the wide range of plant and animal species we see around us.

The theory itself was relatively simple and short. Most of *The Origin of Species* consisted of examples drawn from Darwin's travel journals, from books and scientific papers, from his correspondence with other scientists, and from his own painstaking experimental work carried out in the gardens and greenhouse or in his study at Down. These examples illustrated and supported every point he made. He described ways in which organisms differ from each other, how they improve to fit their environment more closely, and how **organs** as well as organisms change their function and evolve. He discussed the fossil record, the evidence to be gained from the study of **embryos** and varying stages of growth (young animals of different species often resemble each other more closely than do their parents, pointing clearly to their common ancestry), and he showed the importance of studying **rudimentary organs** that had changed their function altogether in the course of evolution.

The first edition of *The Origin of Species* sold out immediately and Darwin straightaway began preparing for revised future editions. "How extremely stupid not to have thought of that," said Thomas Henry

Thomas Henry Huxley, the young zoologist who reviewed **The Origin of Species** and defended its ideas against all opposition. Friends called him "Darwin's bulldog," because of his vigorous attacks on the clergy and others who opposed Darwinism.

Huxley, a brilliant young biologist who reviewed *The Origin* favorably for *The London Times*. Huxley was a lively, aggressive and effective popularizer of science. He became a staunch defender of Darwin's theory as well as a close friend. Defenders were needed, for attacks against Darwin, in the press and at scientific meetings, were gaining in momentum.

THE OXFORD EVOLUTION DEBATE

In June 1860, seven months after the publication of *The Origin of Species*, a famous confrontation occurred between those who supported Darwin's theory and those who opposed it. The event was a debate sponsored by the British Association for the Advancement of Science, held at England's prestigious Oxford University.

Opponents of Darwin's theory chose as their chief spokesperson a highly respected religious leader, the Reverend Samuel Wilberforce, who was the Anglican bishop of Oxford and was known as a great public speaker. The bishop had little naturalistic background, so an influential naturalist named Richard Owen helped prepare him for the debate. Owen, who was famous for his work with dinosaurs, had talked at length with Darwin after publication of the theory, but disagreed with Darwin's conclusions. Darwin's health was not good and he could not attend, so his friends Thomas Henry Huxley and Joseph Dalton Hooker prepared to go to Oxford and defend his theory. Chairman of the event was Darwin's former mentor from Cambridge, John Henslow.

More than 700 people showed up at the Oxford University library to hear the discussion. Wilberforce spoke first. Following Owen's advice, he tried to trivialize Darwin's ideas. In a famous exchange, the bishop scathingly asked Huxley on which side of his family—his grandfather's or grandmother's—did he claim descent from apes? Huxley replied

Evolution Under Attack

"Absurd facts ... utterly rotten fabric of guesswork and speculation," spluttered one review. "Contradicts the revealed relation of the Creation to the Creator," said another more soberly. Darwin had carefully left out most references to man's evolution, hoping that his case for the rest of creation

that he would rather be descended on both sides from apes, than from a man who misused his "great gifts" of intelligence to obscure the truth.

Several others spoke during the debate as well, including Darwin's former *Beagle* shipmate Captain Robert FitzRoy, who denounced the book and implored the crowd to believe in the Bible. Finally, Darwin's friend Joseph Hooker stood to speak. The famous botanist spent nearly two hours refuting all of the arguments against Darwin's theory while clearly explaining the main ideas.

Bishop Samuel Wilberforce, a brilliant orator and leading churchman who opposed Darwin's theory.

Following the Oxford evolution debate, both sides claimed victory. However, in time most people came to consider this event as a major victory for the supporters of Darwin's theory about evolution through natural selection.

PROF. DARWIN.

This is the ape of form.

Love's Labor Lost, act 5, scene 2.

Some four or five descents since.

All's Well that Ends Well, act 3, sc. 7.

One of many cartoons published when Darwin's ideas of man's evolution from ape-like ancestors became known. It shows Darwin comparing himself with a monkey friend in a hand mirror.

would be judged on its merits alone. He was nevertheless attacked for his unspoken belief that man is descended from apelike ancestors—and just as vigorously defended by Huxley and other scientific supporters. Many of Darwin's attackers were Christians, among them the bishop of Oxford, Samuel Wilberforce.

Although Darwin was clearly offering an alternative to the Bible in his account of the origins of species, he was still a religious man and did not exclude a Creator from his theory. "Thus from the war of nature, from famine and death," he wrote at the end of his book "... the production of the higher animals, directly follows. There is grandeur in this view of life, with its several powers, having been originally breathed by the Creator into a few forms or into one; and that ... from so simple a beginning endless forms most beautiful and most wonderful have been, and are being evolved."

This wholly reverent view of Creation did not prevent churchmen, fellow scientists, and laymen (even Robert FitzRoy, his old sparring-partner from the *Beagle*) from attacking him as being ungodly. To some people it seemed that Darwin was opposing holy writ. Others were appalled by his notion that chance—chance variations, chance selection—was playing so important a part in the process. Darwin might believe in God, but it could not be a benevolent God who had started the process of evolution and left it to run its course.

If Darwin was right, then much else was wrong—in society, in industry, and in every walk of life. Man, not God, was responsible for his fate; man must take responsibility for the society he had created. No liberally minded person who accepted Darwin's theory could believe, for example, that poverty and other social injustices were sent by God and had to be tolerated; they were man-made and had to be put right. And what of this struggle for existence—does the Law of the Jungle prevail, and shall it prevail in our society? The churchmen thundered from the pulpits, the scientists pontificated, the arguments rolled back and forth in Britain and across the world.

Darwin left the debating to those who enjoyed it and got on with his work quietly. He seldom appeared in public, preferring the peace of his home at Downe and the happiness of his family life. He and Emma had seven bright and intelligent children whose company he enjoyed far more than the hubbub of scientific meetings. His health was still a constant problem, but by living quietly and working in a regular routine, he achieved an extraordinary output of scientific studies. He wrote about orchids, climbing plants, fertilization of plants, and a major study of variation in animals and plants under domestication. Then in 1871 came *The Descent of Man and Selection in Relation to Sex*, which stated firmly what *The Origin of Species* had left unsaid—that man too is a product of evolution and not a special creation. Again controversy raged. But Darwin, now aged 62, was happy to ignore it all. Life was short, and he still had important work to complete.

TEXT-DEPENDENT QUESTIONS

1. Which two friends did Darwin ask to review Alfred Russel Wallace's paper on evolution?
2. When was *The Origin of Species* published?
3. What was Darwin's second major publication on evolution, in 1871?

RESEARCH PROJECT

Using your school library or the internet, research one of the following nineteenth-century scientists who interacted with Darwin: Charles Lyell, Joseph Dalton Hooker, or Richard Owen. Write a two-page paper about this scientist's work and career accomplishments, and present it to your class.

Photo of Charles Darwin, taken in 1868. As an older man, he still took regular walks in the lanes about his home, and was actively interested in many aspects of biology, from earthworms to orchids.

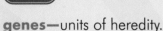

WORDS TO UNDERSTAND

genes—units of heredity.

insectivorous plants—plants that are able to capture and digest insects, such as the Venus flytrap.

questionnaire—a set of written questions with a choice of answers, devised for the purpose of a survey or statistical study.

CHAPTER 6

Finale

Darwin continued to study and write throughout the last decade of his life. His health improved slightly after publication of *The Descent of Man*, and his final years were happy ones. In 1872 he published *The Expression of the Emotions in Man and Animals*, an idea that he had originally intended to fill no more than a single chapter in *The Descent of Man*. For this book he drew heavily on his own observations of his children and domestic animals, including his pet sheepdog Bob. He also found information in the local lunatic asylum, in zoos, and in his own excellent library. He circulated **questionnaires** to his overseas correspondents to discover how widespread around the world were smiles, frowns, shoulder shrugging, kissing, and other indications of human emotions. He also tried to relate the expressions of man to those of apes and monkeys.

Then followed three more major studies of plants—the biology of **insectivorous plants** in 1875, and two works on mechanisms of fertilization in 1876 and 1877. His last great work was published in 1881, the year before he died. It was a detailed study of earthworms—a development of a short paper he had written many years before describing the effects of earthworms in churning up, re-distributing and improving soils.

To collect the data for his book, Darwin as usual studied his subject minutely, counting wormcasts on lawns and in fields, examining the detailed structure of both the casts and the animals that made them, and keeping earthworms in jars on the desk in his study. He stalked them at

A page from **The Expression of the Emotions in Man and Animals**, *Darwin's third major work on evolution. The book was published in 1872.*

midnight to discover their reactions to light, played the bassoon and piano to them to check their responses to vibrations of different frequencies, and calculated the amount of soil they transported in different situations. On the downs near his home, for example, they brought up to the surface an astonishing 18 tonnes of soil per acre each year. He concluded that earthworms were responsible, too, for the sinking of Stonehenge, the collapse of large buildings with poor foundations, and the burying of Roman pavements.

Like the rest of his books, *Formation of Vegetable Mould* collected together simple observations of a kind that almost anyone could make, and arranged them in ways that brought out unsuspected or half-suspected truths. The gift of simplicity was Darwin's genius; no observation was too trivial to record, no plant or animal too humble to notice, to study and to learn from. On this gift is based the lasting value of his work, for his books are still read with interest by scientists today, and his conclusions—formed over a century ago—often

Darwin's comfortable study at Down House, where most of his writing was done.

suggest new lines of research and inquiry for modern students.

Natural selection is still the most fertile ground for scientific research. Since Darwin's time, whole new fields of inquiry have developed to throw further light on how natural selection works. Although natural selection is easy to understand, it is still difficult to demonstrate in action. Darwin knew nothing of **genes** or the principles of Mendelian inheritance, which came to light after his time. He would have been delighted by Mendel's simple research on garden peas, and astonished to see the scope—and the relevance to his own research—of the vast science of genetics that has now arisen from it. He would perhaps be amused to find scientists still arguing—as they did in his day—over definitions of "species" and other basic concepts. He

Drawing of Charles Darwin made in 1880, two years before the scientist's death.

could not fail to be pleased that every biologist is now basically a Darwinist, and that the concept of evolution—slow, gradual change for the better—has replaced the concept of special creation and status quo (the existing state of affairs) in almost every walk of life.

Charles Darwin died peacefully at his home in Downe on April 19, 1882, deeply loved by his family and honored by his scientific colleagues. He was buried close to Isaac Newton in Westminster Abbey.

Scan here to watch a short biography of Charles Darwin:

CHARLES DARWIN

'Freedom of thought is best promoted by the gradual illumination
of men's minds, which follows from the advance of science.'
Charles Robert Darwin (1809–1882)

TEXT-DEPENDENT QUESTIONS

1. What book did Darwin publish in 1872?
2. What was Darwin's final great work, published in 1881?
3. Where is Charles Darwin buried?

 ## RESEARCH PROJECT

When Darwin published his theory of natural selection, he created an uproar. To this day, the subject of evolution provokes debate in many communities. Using the local library or the internet, find out about some important court cases that deal with the teaching of evolution and its religious-based alternatives, such as creationism or intelligent design. These could include the 1925 Scopes trial in Tennessee, or more recent federal court cases like *Webster v. New Lenox School District* (1990) or *Kitzmiller v. Dover* (2005). Do some research on both sides of the case, and write a two-page summary that can be presented to your class.

Chronology

1809

Charles Darwin is born in Shrewsbury, England, on February 12.

1818

Started school in Shrewsbury; mother died.

1825

Medical studies began at Edinburgh University.

1827

Commenced theology studies at Cambridge University.

1831

Graduated from Cambridge University; met Captain FitzRoy, and embarked from Plymouth on H.M.S. *Beagle*.

1832

Visited Cape Verde Islands, Rio de Janeiro, Montevideo, Tierra del Fuego.

1833

Sailed to Falkland Islands; made excursions into Patagonia.

1834

Visited Chile and Peru, climbed in the Andes.

1835

Experienced earthquake in Chile and visited Galápagos Islands.

1836

Homeward voyage via Tahiti, New Zealand, Australia, Cocos Islands; home to England.

Statue of Charles Darwin in front of the library in Shrewsbury, England.

1837

Commenced writing notebooks on evolution.

1839

Marriage; *Beagle* journals published.

1842

Moved to Down House, Kent.

1844

Draft of *Origin of Species* written.

1858

Letter on origin of species received from Wallace.

1859

On the Origin of Species by Means of Natural Selection published.

1862

The Various Contrivances by which Orchids are Fertilized by Insects published.

1868

The Variation of Animals and Plants under Domestication published.

1871

The Descent of Man, and Selection in Relation to Sex published.

1872

The Expression of the Emotions in Man and Animals Published

1881

The Formation of Vegetable Mould through the Action of Worms published.

1882

Died at Down House on April 19.

The Charles Darwin Research Station on Santa Cruz Island, part of the Galápagos chain, is used to conduct scientific research.

BIENVENIDOS — WELCOME

ESTACION CIENTIFICA
CHARLES DARWIN
Charles Darwin Research Station

Further Reading

Bortz, Fred. *Charles Darwin and the Theory of Evolution by Natural Selection.* New York: Rosen, 2014.

Lieberman, Philip. *The Theory that Changed Everything: "On the Origin of Species" as a Work in Progress.* New York: Columbia University Press, 2018.

Morus, Iwan Rhys. *The Oxford Illustrated History of Science.* New York: Oxford University Press, 2017.

Nardo, Don. *The Importance of Charles Darwin.* Farmington Hills, Mich.: Lucent Books, 2005.

Sis, Peter. *The Tree of Life: Charles Darwin.* New York: Farrar, Straus, and Giroux, 2003.

Wootton, David. *The Invention of Science: A New History of the Scientific Revolution.* New York: Harper Perennial, 2016.

Quammen, Peter. *The Reluctant Mr. Darwin: An Intimate Portrait of Charles Darwin and the Making of His Theory of Evolution.* New York: Atlas Books, 2007.

Internet Resources

www.darwins-theory-of-evolution.com

This website provide an overview of Darwin's theory of evolution, with links to articles and videos that help to explain the theory.

www.aboutdarwin.com

A useful, well-organized site that provides links to facts about Charles Darwin's ideas and writings.

www.galapagos.org

This fascinating and educational site promotes conservation and scientific research and education, especially in the Galápagos Islands, where Darwin first saw clear evidence of evolution in action.

www.sciencenewsforstudents.org

Science News for Students is an award-winning online publication dedicated to providing age-appropriate, topical science news to learners, parents and educators.

www.pbs.org/wgbh/nova

The website of NOVA, a science series that airs on PBS. The series produces in-depth science programming on a variety of topics, from the latest breakthroughs in technology to the deepest mysteries of the natural world.

http://evolution.berkeley.edu/evolibrary/article/evo_01

This website, sponsored by the University of California at Berkeley, provides an introduction to evolution and the origins of life.

Influences and ideas

Darwin did not conceive his natural selection in a vacuu imagination. Some of the mo out here.

The age of the earth

Writing the history of the earth

In 1774, the **Comte de Buffon** estimated that the earth was at least 75,000 years old.

By 1800, educated people generally accepted that the earth was very old, although its exact age was the subject of much debate. This allowed time for great geological change to happen gradually.

The Cambridge professor of geology Reverend Adam Sedgwick (1785–1873) believed in divine creation and was passionately opposed to the concept of evolution of species.

He thought that there had been a series of cataclysmic events which had shaped the earth's crust; this explained why some creatures now found as fossils had become extinct. He introduced the 22-year-old Darwin to geology, taking him on a field trip to Wales.

Charles Lyell (1797–1875) was a geologist who thought gradual change was more important than sudden changes in shaping the earth's crust. He argued that the processes acting in the past were no different from and no more intense than the ones that we can see around us today.

Darwin applied Lyell's ideas to the places he saw during his voyage on the *Beagle*. The two eventually became close friends.

A visitor to Down House looks at an exhibition on Darwin's contribution to scientific understanding.

Series Glossary of Key Terms

anomaly—something that differs from the expectations generated by an established scientific idea. Anomalous observations may inspire scientists to reconsider, modify, or come up with alternatives to an accepted theory or hypothesis.

evidence—test results and/or observations that may either help support or help refute a scientific idea. In general, raw data are considered evidence only once they have been interpreted in a way that reflects on the accuracy of a scientific idea.

experiment—a scientific test that involves manipulating some factor or factors in a system in order to see how those changes affect the outcome or behavior of the system.

hypothesis—a proposed explanation for a fairly narrow set of phenomena, usually based on prior experience, scientific background knowledge, preliminary observations, and logic.

natural world—all the components of the physical universe, as well as the natural forces at work on those things.

objective—to consider and represent facts without being influenced by biases, opinions, or emotions. Scientists strive to be objective, not subjective, in their reasoning about scientific issues.

observe—to note, record, or attend to a result, occurrence, or phenomenon.

science—knowledge of the natural world, as well as the process through which that knowledge is built through testing ideas with evidence gathered from the natural world.

subjective—referring to something that is influenced by biases, opinions, and/or emotions. Scientists strive to be objective, not subjective, in their reasoning about scientific issues.

test—an observation or experiment that could provide evidence regarding the accuracy of a scientific idea. Testing involves figuring out what one would expect to observe if an idea were correct and comparing that expectation to what one actually observes.

theory—a broad, natural explanation for a wide range of phenomena in science. Theories are concise, coherent, systematic, predictive, and broadly applicable, often integrating and generalizing many hypotheses. Theories accepted by the scientific community are generally strongly supported by many different lines of evidence. However, theories may be modified or overturned as new evidence is discovered.

HOMO
NEANDERTHALIS

HOMO
ANTECESSOR

HOMO
SAPIENS

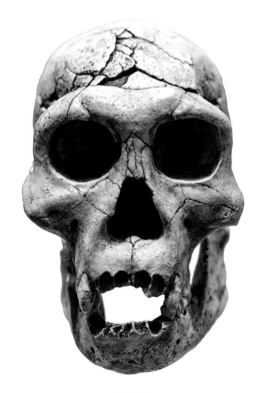

HOMO
ERECTUS

Index

About the Author

Bradley Sneddon is a graduate of the University of Delaware. He teaches biology in Newark, Delaware, where he lives with his wife and their two dogs. This is his first book.

Photo Credits